PIKI AKE!

PIKI AKE!
Poems 1990-92

Robert Sullivan

AUCKLAND UNIVERSITY PRESS

First published 1993
Auckland University Press
University of Auckland
Private Bag 92019
Auckland

© Robert Sullivan 1993

This book is copyright. Apart from fair dealing for the purpose of
private study, research, criticism, or review, as permitted under the
Copyright Act, no part may be reproduced by any process without the prior permission of
Auckland University Press.

ISBN 1 86940 084 4

Typeset in Garamond
Printed by GP Print Ltd, Wellington

Published with the assistance of the
Literature Committee of the
Queen Elizabeth II Arts Council

Distributed outside New Zealand
by Oxford University Press

Contents

Maui Tosses the Hook 1
Listen to the Rhythm of the Falling Rain 2
The Prophet Rua 3
Karakia 5
Shadow of the Land 6
The Business Ethic 7
Maori are Children of God 9
MANA 11
Wedding 12
Taupiri 13
Doing it 14
Space 1992 15
Reading 16
Drive 17
Separation 18
Huh 19
Waitomo 21
Freefall 22
The Poet Kisses . . . 23
Outside Inside 24
Arch Hill 25
May Day 27
He Looks with Fondness 28

Harawene Whanau Reunion
Kaupapa of our Reunion 31
Sitting in front of the Karetu Marae 33
Te Hokinga Mai 34
City 35
Monday 36
Tuesday 37
Christmas Day 38

Boxing Day 39
Friday 40
The Unveiling 41
Falling 42
Working Committee 43

Work 44

The George Grey Room
Stations of the Cross 45
The Private Press 46
Conservation 47
Job Description 48
Vacant Situation 49
Take Care 50
Other Works Consulted 51
The Real Thing 52
On Display 53
On the Road Again 54
Getting There 55
Sole Charge 56
Sir George 57
The Onehunga Rare Books Assistant 58

To Anne

Robert wishes to thank
Michele Leggott for her help,
Sue Tetai (kia ora, cuz)
and also the QEII Arts Council for a New Writers grant.
Thanks to Robin Morrison for back cover photo.

Maui Tosses the Hook

Tangaroa
make your sea lie smooth
           as greenstone
aid the flight of my bone
gentle your friend the summer wind
so he casts like whakapapa
from the mouths of tohunga
              make the line taut
                the hook unyielding
     pull it on
     pull it strong
make Te-Ika-a-Maui come!

Listen to the Rhythm of the Falling Rain

You, her and him, are in this —
it is a jug of pure water in the likeness
of a virgin glazed with rain beside white
chickens, or a mountain pinned to a railway

station (an installation), and in this way
the rain courses through holies, idols,
people of pain and passion, chance rain
that bends heads with its drops, dissolves,

shatters light, carries logs in bending streams.
Men and women scramble to dam the wondrous rain.
They cannot understand its massive rhythm:
that such a cascade feeds on joy and not

on competition. It is grace that sets
sun moon and stars to shine. Laughter
comes from talking, pain from healing.
Rain moves the strongest hearts.

The Prophet Rua

Rua. Housed in the Waikato amongst
the taonga of that people. Looking
through a glass installation at the river,
dirty now, but the people remain. One

of them stands beside the waka commissioned
by Princess Te Puea, a revered mother of all
Maori people. I am quiet. My Pakeha friends have
left me to consider this exhibition on my own,

which gives me time and space to wander. I look
at him, but cannot say I am Ngapuhi, which is my own
self-judgement. One of my tupuna, it is rumoured,
ended his life in this land; they skinned

his intricately carved buttocks, covered
a calabash with them, took his tongue,
used it for the handle, boiled the rest, poured
him in, rowed to the middle of a lake and threw it.

His descendants still pay for the rumoured myths.
I leave the Waikato exhibits and begin the journey
to the land of Urewera, Tuhoe, the people,
the Ringatu faith, the people of Rua and peace.

They have erected a large-scale house of cards,
there is talk of Rua's imprisonment for not
holding a liquor licence. The Pakeha
trump up the charge — they want Rua to fight.

There is a recording of the policemen
who arrested Rua saying excessive force
was used. There is a poem by David Eggleton,
artwork by Ralph Hotere. Many artists

focus on the community he created, in photos,
sculpture, Rua is important. I really am
an Auckland tourist. My chest is hot and filled.
I am speechless with knowledge. My tongue is out.

Karakia
for Bruce Stewart

I touch Papatuanuku my earthmother
      give hands up to Ranginui
my skyfather
      then beat both wings of the heart
skull it down through the pelvis
to a rosewater bowl
filling with stones: chance/angst/loneliness/failure
dip hands in this sprinkle
          heads in clarity pass the speech of people on
blush and touch make love slowly (be careful)

we slide in a round of writhing
weeds that thrash a jive
expressed in a loud way (I'm out of my circle)
persevere beat your heart's wings
          fly out to greet them
shout 'Hii!' (hee) to the ground
shout 'Haa!' to the sky
through veins people give and take
      fine as those crossing a petal
      floating on a bowl
health to you brother (we hongi)
      health to you sister (we kiss)
splash your paddles
breathe deeply drink up
we've got a chant of unbroken
          tone/s to toast!
a meeting on respected grounds
an open sound so pure it shakes the host

Shadow of the Land
for Allen Curnow

This is where the body meets the land.
McCahon McCahon McCahon so holy.
Holiness and vulnerability. I will
lie with the land in my single bed.
We are trapped for fear of turning.

Turn around, face the yellow eye
of day, stretch the point out. Let
an old man's horizon be a window,
a dammed reservoir of vision that splits
the land into a literature of prisms.

The glittering eye of the minor prism
flies with the tui, bends, separates
in the way of a river valley, and in the way
of the wind as it curls froth from waves,
or spies a face emerging from wild surf.

The prevailing prism is a westerly
hitting the massive host. It is focused
on the coast. It is a wonder the land
remains. The prism's lines are distinct,
a mountain of black sand, a shadowland.

Hawaiki is to be found in its blue night.
Hawaiki is just hidden from sight.
Hawaiki is in the wealth of time.
Hawaiki is a yawn and a stretch from life.
Hawaiki is deep it lasts it is desire.

The Business Ethic
for Hone

Thoughts range to the Whangamata rise
with its tree plucking eyes, a tad Goth
Austro-Kiwian alps spearing white
waves where sand bars stave the rave,

heading to ground, thinking of exotica
kissing deck, needles spread; our legs
trestle — yeah, that stiff — the odd patch
where the dirt sinks into pools, slides

that are slushy skids, wet tread.
One day this will get sucked out, a big pucker
and the ageing pohutukawas on the shoreline,
the toss between GRI or ripe pines

and tears from blinking to pinch
this corner, that bay, for resort chains,
will all go up the blow-hole, the last straw,
the big gurgler. A vestige of an Access scheme

is a lone bench beneath a black-necked
pohutukawa; it's a possum rip seesaw
the owners have just familiarised
with the white sand (hey bud!)

seen the cave which fills at high water
been briefed on a crack at the top where
the water would spit at them and between
nibbles are impressed by the cakey texture

the gullet shape the grotto
they admire the brown trickle
begin to think of giant trees and moas
they start licking their chops

agree it has a salty taste
(passed) that the motion of the sea
is incredible for something that's supposed
to be dead (unanimous) like falling trees.

Maori are Children of God

Somewhere in the land's mind a taniwha
lifts his head and grins, a mountain
walks off with a female mountain,
a waiata is sung in honour of the above

Maori are children of God

a dead tohunga sees me and I see this
we are talking about the madness
that has taken the people by the sip
in aluminium pints quarts and handles

Maori are children of God

the sickness of the city the iwi's filtered
oration on streets with rap not speech
and the power of their history strong as Edison
or Einstein weaker than the matakite man

Maori are children of God

and soldiers and mercenaries and free people
and makers of villages and makers of waka
and breathers of spirit and air and growers
and laughers and artists and the solemn

who represented all these things
of war-peace-food-love-beauty-sleep-
river-ocean-wind-fatherdom-motherdom-
forest-man-woman and the numbered

and should not forget as they live
in this mixture of a time where they are
folded into a document that takes blackness
from dignity and spits/gifts some back.

The Maori are children of God.

```
                              MANA
IOIOIOIOIOIOIOIOIOIOIOIOIOIOIOIOIOIOIOIOIOIOIOIOIOIOIOIO
CELESTIALSPHERETHENIGHTEMBRACEANCESTORSMARAMAFLIGHT
IOIOIOIOIOIOIOIOIOIOIOIOIOIOIOIOIOIOIOIOIOIOIOIOIOIOIOIO

                Goats                  RANGIRANGIRANGIRANGI
                Hill                   TE          TE          TE
    Energy>>>Pa<<<Energy               UA    T     RA    H     PO
                Joy                    TE    A     TE    I     TE
                Intellect              UA    N     RA    N     PO
                                       TE    E     TE    E     TE
        {Big Hairy Structures}         UA          RA          PO
    Iwi Transition:                    PAPAPAPAPAPAPAPAPAPA
    sustainable? achievable?            I     I     I     I     I
    they've got the whole world         T     T     T     T     T
    brush-pube-marram                   O     O     O     O     O
    nurse pollution less kai
    land held tight hold hands         LAND=WHENUA
    te tiriti te mana motuhake!       / MIHI THE LAND
    minds engaged we are             / FIRST!
    sequential seductive            /
    unpopular with the Pakeha      / MANA=RESPECT
        regenerate                /  someone
    the ancestors aloud          /   carries                T
    Ruapekapeka! Ohaeawai!      /    with them              H
    learn your history         /     from their whanau      E
    tino rangatiratanga!      /                             F
      \      /      \        /       THEFTTHEFTTHEFTTHEFT
    ****\**/BUT THEFT!! \ ** /   *****SEVERED********************
         \/             \/                T     R
        DIFFUSION      CONFUSION          E     U
    Light and Anger   Death and Sorrow    W     A
                                          H
           ∴ HUMILIATION                  I
                                          T
        rEVENge  and  ACCEPTance          I
            paths to mana
    TANGATAWHENUATANGATAWHENUATANGATAWHENUATANGATAETU!!
    WARPEACEWARPEACEWARPEACEWARPEACEWARPEACEWARPEACEWAR
    REVENGECOMPENSATIONRETURNDISGUSTFRUSTRATIONHATEAH!!
```

Wedding

I pocket the moment
I pick up their vows and I keep them
as they keep each other now
a woman friend lover a man friend lover
coupled there is shunt no place like it
go to them feel them reach them
to the picture on your wall by William Claxton
Times Square, New York 1960 . . . see how
she leans toward his leaving
and the saxophonist rocks her
playing cents and aisles
life on a payment the pavement

Taupiri

I am at Taupiri Bay, on the spot, here —
where surfers bob, grass bristles and

my friends the lovers kiss. We get charged
$2.00 for beach access. I want to flash

my manaia and shout 'tangata whenua — what's
going on here? make way!' but we still pay

a buck in fifty cent pieces in the honesty
box. Round the corner, as we drive over

the hill, the next beach is free, which
pisses us off, and we swim there too. Every meal

is brown bread honeycomb ham cheese water
runny butter lying on your back your side

or backside then watching him swim in his
underwear or run in his underwear along the beach.

Doing it

We stand at the back of Grandad's house
in the regenerating bush with Drew and Trace.

We stand at the top of a rock which
we climb by wedging ourselves upon flax

and roots of pohutukawa. We crouch
inside that rock in the sea cave where

penguin tracks trail the deeps
and our voices fill the hollow left

by the tide. We glide and stroke in
rock jacuzzis where the tide just reaches

and our shoulders sink into bright saltwater.
I sleep and am woken with a sunburn warning.

Space 1992

me dad Russell Pat Vikki Sharon and Kerry by a king's haul of snapper. The memory slipped into my chest. That's not how to cut oranges boy, my mother says. These memories surprise me, not only my family. One foot over the Hau Moana waiting for the waves to settle so I can get in the dinghy, waiting forever, a crowd of onlookers, I can hear their thoughts: 'will he get in?' A forty-two foot work in ferro cement. Take away the love and the anger. Floating on a determinant. Gills spilling into muscle. Oars' flash. Payment. Payment damn pay me. Payment. Pay. You're grown up now boy. Pick it up. A chess set kicked off a coffee table. A black and blue bum. A girl's skirt lifted in the choir, tears of embarrassment when I'm told off in front of another class. St Peter's wolf cubs at the Anzac Day parade, I'm holding the flag. That's the photo of me outside the Jellicoe Park Pools on Anzac Day. See how I reach for what I cannot have? The cloud poem written about me hunting in the grass looking at a cloud that looks like an alligator. Mrs Naire likes it, asks me to glue cotton wool to the outside. I fold fill and staple it with more wool. I was so proud. She hung it from the classroom ceiling. Watch about you boy. You're in another room. This one has a computer and a printer and a single bed. You're looking at logos of William Claxton and Napoleon brandy. The tape deck is playing Kate Bush. You have a cold, have eaten an overripe orange, dry, you want to go back. I want to go back. I am filling another disk with this. Hello. I know what you've been dreaming. It's a pleasure to select your text. Pick it up. Hello. Mate I know that you're ill. Take the day off work. Work/work? [work] Anne writes: I hope you're dealing with the difference between work and Work. Press return. Huh? uh. My head. The desire of the text, to be desired by text, to write another edition of the text of desire. This is between him and his chest.

Reading

        morning in Tauranga
                lunch off the Waikato
(before the Rua Kenana exhibition)
          afternoon tea here at the place of no
names and as sea cajoles me over rocks
            straight out of the mouth
                sea sparkle below
Reeboks JAG MEN borrowed T-shirt togs and loaned
blues brother glasses I see
            a grey moth
            a white butterfly
and read the Stage I NZ Lit assignment
      —Jenny's boyfriend
        my last year
        Fleur down south
    sweet Mary's voice
        Bob at another launch
        Hone's elegy —
                then sniff up the woodsmoke
                look down this cliff and
                consider
      a massive sprawled weekend
been filled and fed and slept
      walked through caves wreathed in spinnerets
        listened to heaps
                of Aretha from the '60s
    '70s funky women Nina Simone
partied up large with strangers
    yet locals
            and that makes them familiar
                they know who I'm with

Drive

minimal conversation
atheistic by arrangement
                                  two cups
of coffee
          tables chairs
and faces waving
at luxuriant courtyard
flax palms maidenhair ferns
noting an epiphyte
                     from biology
he cannot explain
the thrill and the lift
of this
      simpleness
being simple
so archaic
          nor the ache
at thinking a late
explanation
              he likes this
yet unsure
wants to 'stick around'
and when they reach
                  her car
the poor boy's pride
twists inside
wanting so much
being so poor
                  at least
to touch as the ache tells
him to run for the one
he just left
              and misses

Separation

On Sunday
when the bells rang
      from St Joseph's
Grey Lynn
      I put my face
in a towel
let it drape the length
of my body
      for warmth

Huh

Candle
light frame
prop darkness
tear

edge
thin wedge
a letter
long

mist
missed
mits

drop
two drops
stop this

camber of
a cameo ambling
caper to cater
to

oh
sign me on
at ten a.m. under
growth

Glenn Miller
six five oh oh oh
throw a punch
take a spill

lash
and splice
to our street
a

little brown jug
of gravy
on our
table

Waitomo

Chaka Khan sings deep through
the hills of Bombay coming back
from Tauranga and Waitomo where

bit of a story to tell . . .
we watched stalagmites
and stalactites of the night calling

this one's the elephant and
that looks like Tina Turner's hairdo
he said I will never forget

the spinnerets dangling
hundreds instead of thousands
the boatman using no oars

just tow lines slung from one side
of the cave to the other and we get
dripped on and if we stood still

didn't swing we'd become pinnacles
but movement is a beast counts its fingers
drives you home hugs you says goodbye

Freefall

in the big sliding window of my room
it is approaching dusk
against a dusty sky

lapis lazuli stuffing
eggshell powder clouds
the parachutes dropping

I cannot see the fallers
they might be plastic
I just see the strings

tugging furiously making
for the Western Springs stadium
or is it the lake I visit

to be calmed by nature
tame swans gentle geese
children laying up adventures

The poet
kisses
an inner
wrist.

Outside Inside

a drop of pink paint
Dulux too tiny
               to call
    a stalagmite nor its pink satellites such signs
   of a shower of home making against a backyard window
passionfruit picking on the old swing and slide

swing me high swing me higher
lean backward on the up
and forward going down
                    have a fight
                    squeeze an ant
sit in the grass and draw
the latest spaceship
                  think a bit
see how the passionfruit
flowers look
like jellyfish
        peach in existence the magnolia competes
     with the small fir
                  rust and gull crap
   mottle the great
   black barbecue plate
            accidental in expanse
                  a talking point
          of fruit through our windows
and as detail slides
lights shinny the gap
              prick soft fabric
          day's vellum
so ancient a close
         finger prints
        in the glowing
      of stardust
what luck to assemble
in this light.

Arch Hill

The first time I've lived near the city
since I was seven, Newmarket Primary and
all that, but there is no domain, just
a tightly clipped field at the foot of
our street beside the North-Western
Motorway. Our backyard looks like the straw

of last week's big top, our neighbours
are seven young male students who've
just come over with beers they lugged up
Queen Street, along K' Road and then Great North
to get here, Bond Street. You don't know
how tough it is to carry four dozen

this far, they said, as I drank another
can. Hang on man, I said, this discussion
is incredibly esoteric and we're living
in one of the poorest areas of Auckland!
There are no barbies, or wooden fences
holding a uniquely landscaped pool,

deck chairs round a cognac, latest lycra
fluttering from the line, John Dory and fries
wrapped in last month's *Metro*, where exercise
consists of practising tongue extensions,
the imaginary acted prattle this Arch Hill resident
despises. And to the real? corrugated fences

that blow with every wish, daytime with
'The Bats', night-time with BFM at eleven, bass
guitar practice at three, five hours' sleep
with the bathroom locked, but we're better off
this way they sing. Our Polynesian neighbours
are very quiet — the teenagers walk the streets

each night — so now I feel a little guilty
the Samoans next door to us in Onehunga were so
loud and that we grumbled and gave them the evils.
Playing with my youngest flatmate's grouse
though, she can swing upside down from
the clothesline and sing row row row

your boat and I'm teaching her chess, and well . . .
poetry. Of course the best advantage is that
I can visit all my friends from here.

May Day

at lunchtime today
they unfurled the Red Flag
the real thing not the song
out at the band rotunda in Albert Park
there were speeches by Jim Knox ex-head
of the F.O.L. and another old timer
who'd been in the lockout of 1951
a lot of people were listening
to the stories of parents shaking
in despair
unemployed workers who had much pain
to bear
there was a lot of swearing and even
a mention of the P.M. crawling up a trouser leg
to wipe the arse of Washington
Ruth spending nine hundred bucks a week
on an apartment
then a cut back to the dole cut
yesterday thirty thousand people
marched up Queen Street
like old times the speaker said
and he got stuck into the Labour Party
to be fair
as I said a lot of people listened
he had a lot to say
I was eating a steak pie and a carton of chips
which I finished in good time

He Looks with Fondness

Stared at the postcard stuck to the wall. Kiri Te Kanawa, a moa, a marae and Mt Taranaki in the background, and the bold lettering, NIGEL BROWN. Stared at the letter from Boston from a childhood penfriend who he shared his life with, and needs to send another letter to. His name is Dermot and he was brought up in Dublin, Ireland.

Troubled times in his head. Troubles spread everywhere. He spread them between the cheese and the ham and eggs. Better. He took his jersey off and felt the ruffles in his shirt. The grey shirt that was once his best. Thought of the people who'd removed it from him, thought of the loves and friends, of the flat in Onehunga where the roaches and the dust held them in together. Other addresses. They rise like shaken scent.

He starts to shake. It is laughter he's shaking with? Is it sorrow? Why is he shaking?

It comes out from the top to the bottom. It leaves him in yellow phlegmy trails that only he can trace. The old emotions leave their trenches and their craters. He needs reshaping.

He watches the teacher from the letters and he copies her abecedarian. What follows.

Is. A fondness is too subjective. How can the objective be served by irrelevant twitterings in the twigs eh? What are the leaves shaking around for except to get their pint of space and earn a keep eh? He propped his elbow on the bar like a log.

Fires he's lit. Fires on islands in the Hauraki Gulf, fires in the Bay of Islands, fires that cooked pipis, smoked snappers, burnt sausages, sweetened steak, fires that propped billies, stoked stories, and the buried fires of touch.

He returns to his returns. Begins his begin.

*************************** **BATONS UP!!!!!** ***************************
SATURDAY 12TH OCTOBER 1 PM. MANUKAU INTERMEDIATE SCHOOL HALL, 74 SYMONDS STREET ONEHUNGA, AUCKLAND. PROCEEDS WILL GO TO THE HARAWENE WHANAU REUNION FOR CHRISTMAS IN THE BAY OF ISLANDS.
********************* **ALL WELCOME! HAERE MAI!** *********************

*************************** **BATONS UP!!!!!** ***************************
SATURDAY 12TH OCTOBER 1 PM. MANUKAU INTERMEDIATE SCHOOL HALL, 74 SYMONDS STREET ONEHUNGA, AUCKLAND. PROCEEDS WILL GO TO THE HARAWENE WHANAU REUNION FOR CHRISTMAS IN THE BAY OF ISLANDS.
********************* **ALL WELCOME! HAERE MAI!** *********************

*************************** **BATONS UP!!!!!** ***************************
SATURDAY 12TH OCTOBER 1 PM. MANUKAU INTERMEDIATE SCHOOL HALL, 74 SYMONDS STREET ONEHUNGA, AUCKLAND. PROCEEDS WILL GO TO THE HARAWENE WHANAU REUNION FOR CHRISTMAS IN THE BAY OF ISLANDS.
********************* **ALL WELCOME! HAERE MAI!** *********************

*************************** **BATONS UP!!!!!** ***************************
SATURDAY 12TH OCTOBER 1 PM. MANUKAU INTERMEDIATE SCHOOL HALL, 74 SYMONDS STREET ONEHUNGA, AUCKLAND. PROCEEDS WILL GO TO THE HARAWENE WHANAU REUNION FOR CHRISTMAS IN THE BAY OF ISLANDS.
********************* **ALL WELCOME! HAERE MAI!** *********************

*************************** **BATONS UP!!!!!** ***************************
SATURDAY 12TH OCTOBER 1 PM. MANUKAU INTERMEDIATE SCHOOL HALL, 74 SYMONDS STREET ONEHUNGA, AUCKLAND. PROCEEDS WILL GO TO THE HARAWENE WHANAU REUNION FOR CHRISTMAS IN THE BAY OF ISLANDS.
********************* **ALL WELCOME! HAERE MAI!** *********************

*************************** **BATONS UP!!!!!** ***************************
SATURDAY 12TH OCTOBER 1 PM. MANUKAU INTERMEDIATE SCHOOL HALL, 74 SYMONDS STREET ONEHUNGA, AUCKLAND. PROCEEDS WILL GO TO THE HARAWENE WHANAU REUNION FOR CHRISTMAS IN THE BAY OF ISLANDS.
********************* **ALL WELCOME! HAERE MAI!** *********************

*************************** **BATONS UP!!!!!** ***************************
SATURDAY 12TH OCTOBER 1 PM. MANUKAU INTERMEDIATE SCHOOL HALL, 74 SYMONDS STREET ONEHUNGA, AUCKLAND. PROCEEDS WILL GO TO THE HARAWENE WHANAU REUNION FOR CHRISTMAS IN THE BAY OF ISLANDS.
********************* **ALL WELCOME! HAERE MAI!** *********************

Harawene Whanau Reunion
for Auntie Lila, with love

Kaupapa of our Reunion (11/12/91)

                      clouds
                            how colours
                                  break   then weigh
      heaviness of land against airiness of sky
                    say
                          look at that pa there
                          or the river
                              it's Taumarere
with a bone-rock undertow
radical as the best beat
                              keeping the whanau fresh
                  for a smooth shave skinny dip
                      an eel chase
                          to shake
off all the things you hate
                          to splash in water
                          and crack the soul's crust
                    thick as blood coursing paddocks knowing
you are welcome, cousin,
                      welcome! after all the wrongs
                          (they ache) to see Turi
     Auntie Judy and my sisters
          Mattie's new house and Grandad looking well
              (we want this reunion)

Nanny Bella's unveiling and flowers for her grave
the fine work my cousin Helen put into decorating
our Christmas tree
                each decoration has the name
of a Harawene (a Sullivan) sewn on in satin,
how the branches connect to make our family tree,
     our whakapapa, and the aim, our kaupapa,
is that we may know and reach out support
and love one another — that's
       what it's all about.

Sitting in front of the Karetu Marae

Ngati Manu's flag hugs the staff.
Ping pong in the dining hall.

The sun spills light over the hills across
the creek. A horse flicks its tail.

The door to Grandad's house is shut.
Ten goats nuzzle on a higher hill.

A dog rolls in front belly up.
This day fills us: slow breeze in a cloth.

Te Hokinga Mai

Tena ra koutou. We're hiring
a video camera to film our powhiri

at the marae on Monday. I'm busy practising
waiata, the hardest is 'tangi a te ruru . . .'

I've been practising hard to remember not only
to greet the meeting house, the marae and my iwi,

but to point to each as I speak, and to sound
as natural as possible. Nan tells me not

to drag out words, that I'm over-pronounced.
It's koh-rua, not caw-rua, for instance.

I saw a video entitled *How d'ya do Mr Governor*
with a lot of different people saying a lot

of different things about the Treaty. One
of the panel said the Maori way of looking

at the world was that we are who we are because
of our past, and that we take that into the future.

City

Before that. The drive to Waipu Cove
for lunch with my family. I took Vikki,

Auntie Louise, baby Amber, and Sarah up.
We drove up in the City. Aunt thinks

it's a neat little car. After lunch
the whanau from the four winds met

at Bay College, Kawakawa. The powhiri
was low key. We assembled in front of

our marae in Karetu. Uncle J.J. did the mihi.
Kia kaha Rapata, he said. I would have to learn Maori.

Monday

After the powhiri we had some kai
and then some drinks. Everyone drinks

mainly at the back of the marae. My Auntie
Hemo has a guitar and soon all the songs

came out: *What a wonderful world* (Grandad's
favourite), and some others I can't remember.

I sing a few, then turn and talk to my Uncle
Turi. 'How did it go over there?'

Then I said I apologised for the hurts
caused the family by what I wrote, and that

they won't appear again. Great Grandpa Turi's
favourite saying was, *days will tell* . . .

Tuesday

Christmas Eve and not much change. We all sleep
in a tent to the side of the complex. The uncles

and some cousins are preparing the meat in the kitchen,
or peeling spuds. It's beginning to get a bit hot

but things are chilling out. So Turi crams me,
Hemo, Auntie Merle, Bella and Fraser into his

old Valiant without the warrant. There's no cops
around this way. He drives us to the deepest

waterhole he knows and we all jump in, though
I jump last. We're in the middle of one of our

uncles' land, and we come here later to go on
a day tramp. Here is the beginning of the bush

where there is gorse and the sound of insects.
I hide out here and dry myself in a patch of sun.

Christmas Day

The separate families of the Harawene whanau
gather in front of the tree for their photos.

The long tables set with napkins, bottles of bubbly
and fizzy drinks from my childhood, have come back

to visit this place. I remember the weekend
when the marae reopened, and the dance on Saturday

when the air was filled with smoke and the floor
was covered with booze and sweat. Already

some of our elders have left from that time.
The kitchen at the back replaces the old open

fire with electric stoves and a furnace with
a gleaming flue. And the ablution block has

showers and new flush toilets. It's all very
swept up, and it takes a lot of cleaning.

When it comes my turn for the photo I'm in
the back row beside James next to the tree.

Boxing Day

Grandad stays at home this morning on the hill —
his gout's playing up something chronic.

I take him up his feed and a can of Lion Red.
He says he'll have the can, and gives his kai

to Uncle Tangi. Slightly later we take the pickup
full of kids to Paihia. There's kayaks,

sea-tricycles, and Kelly Tarlton's shipwreck museum.
I play Uncle Ed's new space invaders game for a while,

then cross the bridge to Waitangi on my own.
I get right to the porch of the Treaty House,

but then I'm turned away by a guide who says it will
cost me five dollars to stay on the Treaty Grounds.

Don't you know I'm tangata whenua, I think,
but I'm too stuffed to protest and leave. Later that night

we have a karaoke and I play Trivial Pursuit with some
cuzzies. I sang *New York, New York* and *Mack the Knife*.

Friday

Uncle John takes us through
the hills on a tramp to the reservoir.

We follow the creek for three hours.
I lag behind with my uncles aunties

and parents who find it tough going.
We see clearings big enough for houses

and a ponga log whare stuffed with
moss which looks like dope (nope).

We see a course where logs from chutes would
meet the stream. We fall far behind the others.

I keep going on my own till I catch them at the dam —
two logs thrown across each bank (an anticlimax).

Much later to my relief we meet up with my
uncles from Karetu who brought their wheels.

John and a few staunch cousins won't give up.
They jog home on the gravel in the dust.

The Unveiling

Nanny Bella's unveiling is today.
We walk along the dusty road, bend

between the fence wires at the foot of the
cemetery hill, and climb up. Some of us

drive the distance. It's a clear hot day.
The priest unveils the stone with a simple

hymn and ceremony. It looks beautiful.
Nanny's photo looks up at me. I think

of the way she used to say my brother's
name, so happy and loud, I cry.

All the whanau touch her grave out of respect.
Once she was my only Nanny. I turn around.

Someone talks to me about Karetu, 'it's
quite an ugly valley really, but it's special'.

Ugly? I think. I wash my hands at the tap
by the cemetery gate. Then I walk away.

Falling

Felling the forest the old people would
send it hurtling down the hills via chutes

until it hit the stream. They'd release the dam
where water did the rest. It was native timber

that went through the valley. Thousands of years
trussed like chicken for spars and yards.

Think of the funds one log would get for our
marae now! Thousands of dollars. There are a few

still on the ridge, hidden from us by their distance,
they ride the land like great stags with full antlers.

We are given a Clayton's choice: give them the chop,
or sell something else, and you all know what that is!

Working Committee

Our whanau has formed a working party
to create a Harawene Trust. Among its chief

objectives is the provision of a strong
education for all our children. There is much

talk about tourism, and we're even discussing
a constitution to incorporate us as a society.

I feel education is number one on the agenda,
but I worry about the cost of subscription

to become a member. A large number of us
are hard up. Also, have we got the basics right?

Unity should be paramount. We must have money
for tangihanga, and education. That is clear.

Work

walking to work
through corridors that take me to the staffroom
the New Zealand and Pacific Department
walking through Literature Arts and Music
through the Whangamata
or a blackwater cave
I am walking over the viaduct
that links my street to Kingsland
and the Rare Books Room

The George Grey Room

Stations of the Cross

In a medieval manuscript today
I saw the life of Christ

His entry into Jerusalem
washing the feet of the disciples

in a work of Spanish incunabula
I saw the conquistadores in South America

lopping noses off faces cutting hands
and feet burning and staking natives

in a missal completely worked in burnished
gold coloured with plant juices ochres

semi-precious lapis lazuli with blue
and red rubrics four line antiphonals

a full page miniature: THE CRUCIFIXION
the same page (verso) on vellum: GOD THE KING

The Private Press

Wandering through the new acquisitions
that still need cataloguing some major names.

The first English novel, *Euphues and his England*
by Lyly, nicely rebound in morocco. Anne came up once —

before I worked here — to read *Swell*
which I haven't looked at yet. I like very much

our facsimile of Ernest Shackleton's *Aurora
Australis* which was printed in the Antarctic.

The expedition sledded the press down there
with huskies around 1908, bound the limited edition

in packing cases and sealskin. We have an
imitation copy of Turnbull's *Julienne Soup* edition —

I wonder if there's an *Irish Stew* somewhere too.
The frontispiece, the aurora, is an eyecatching blue.

I use this anecdote to emphasise not only the artistry
of printers, but also what an intrepid business it is.

Conservation

Mostly the books need protection
from the damp, from the heat, from any

sudden change. At the moment on display
are rare autographs including one of G. B. Shaw

the scallywag. Many patrons of the library
are included in the collection: Thomas Wilson

Leys, who made Ponsonby a seat of learning
and kick-started the *Auckland Star*, George Grey

of course, as well as little snippets like
Tennyson saying how he fell down in the dark,

'I almost broke my kneepan', one from Queen
Elizabeth II thanking the Mayor of Auckland,

John Allum, for the 'teaspoons tipped with
paua shell' which are a symbol of her subjects'

'loyalty and affection'. There's also a treaty
signed by Cromwell's son Richard, the Lord Protector.

Job Description

Conditions for handling a rare book, even
a medieval manuscript, aren't that strict. If one

is taking notes a pencil should be used, definitely
not a pen, and gloves must be worn while handling

the item. Sometimes the Rare Books staff have to help
explain what's going on in a particular book,

which can be harrowing, but normally we're called on
to prop a book up, or talk about the collection.

The most popular items are the Catholic Missal
and Rossdhu Book of Hours, St Augustine's *De Civitate*

Dei printed 1468, the Josephus *Wars of the Jews*.
I think the most amazing are our Ethiopic manuscripts

with their rare coptic bindings. When I give a talk
I always show John Audubon's two-metre tall *Birds of America*

and the two-centimetre *Schloss's English Bijou Almanac*.
The tallest and the shortest somehow sums it up for them.

Vacant Situation

We have work from other denominations.
Jewish material, the Koran, and even facsimile

editions of an Egyptian Book of the Dead.
I had to stop someone once from using their

watercolour kit and sketchpad and tracing
the hieroglyphs! On occasion, while cleaning the larger

books, I've come across studs from days
when they chained reference books, also

pressed flowers, fern and oak leaves, and on page
four hundred and something of the first volume of

the 1638 *Book of Martyrs* a yellow bookmark on which
is scribbled 'do not remove this — being read'

and it is undated. Although it's a church
book, I don't think the woodcuts in *Ars Moriendi*,

or *The Art of Dying*, are very Christian. The
last woodcut is of an angel of judgement holding

two bowls of people dangling from scales, one up
one down, how people were hired and fired then.

Take Care

How can I redeem this posh tone against the foreground
of my own small reality? where is the suffering artist,

Curnow's guilt, Baxter's ghost, the best and the worst
of it? how can I risk assertion, expose myself to

my working-class roots without getting nuked? exclusive,
élitist, material, consumptive, but good honest work.

Calfskin for vellum would be soaked in lime, hair scraped
off, scrubbed smooth with pumice, scribes and students

would use goose quills dipped in lamp black; many herds
of sheep and cattle ended up at the book works.

Well I'd rather be burnished than a bit of gristle.
Today the paper coughs-up-yellow at a hint of a glimmer.

Other Works Consulted

A book on wild horses and dancing turkeys for sale
in a trade catalogue I was indexing today

a lot of twentieth-century fiction
also got a stock list from Pickering & Chatto

(Lord & Lady Rees-Mogg directors)
of eighteenth-century literature

walked into the safe for someone wanting
to see the First Folio (1623) and our

William Blake prophecies, *Europe* and *America*,
printed at Lambeth around 1794. Last night

me and my flatmates listened to a tape
of some Southern hog-calling. The real thing.

The Real Thing

The Duke of Burgundy's coats of arms
have been skilfully removed from

the border decorations of our *Missale*.
He was deemed a traitor, then rubbed out.

Blake's method of deep relief etching
on copper was a mystery until World War II.

His illustrations to the *Divine Comedy*,
Young's *Night Thoughts* and Blair's *The Grave*

are incredible. I wish I could do that.
I watched a video in the Audio-Visual Library

with Japanese subtitles called *A Blake Celebration*
and they had this dude waltzing through fields

hugging lots of children and singing. After Baxter
it's hard to believe, but that was Blake all over.

On Display

In the Travel Display we showed *Headhunters
of Borneo* and the journal of Joseph Banks.

Best bits of that display were the Africa cabinets
with Speke Stanley Livingstone hamming it up: 'the sound

of trumpets, and the Totties were off!' (Speke).
Grey's explorations through Western Australia

were also of interest, though he seldom wrote
an original thing here. Autograph Letters features

a strongman known as the 'Patagonian Sampson'
of Sadlers Wells — Giovanni Belzoni, and William

Colenso who printed the first book in New Zealand,
Ko te Rongo Pai, but the first press was that of William

Yate, who printed New Zealand's first booklet.
There's also a letter from von Tempsky outlining a massacre.

Recently, a man came in with a Sotheby's sale price
on our scrappy 1813 edition, inscribed by Grey,

of a book on Australian birds, a previously unknown copy.
It's worth 250,000 pounds! So I put it in the safe.

On the Road Again

When I started in the Auckland Public Library service
I held a job on relief staff. I'd move from library

to library, relieving at the busiest or short-staffed
libraries. I remember one of the first conversations

I had with a fellow library assistant was about the criteria
for employment. If a man applied for a job, they'd

always say, 'ooh a man', and she was smirking. All
us pool staff have our favourite places, mine was Epsom.

It's the place where I first held a light pen,
and a librarian there said it was a good idea

to read the covers of books while you're
wanding them so that you look interested. Good tip.

Once I worked in Central and helped a security guard
wrestle a man to the floor — the man said I had better

manners than the guard. He was banned later, but the
circulation people said he was a regular, who had bleeding

gums and was a drunk. A lot of vagabonds sleep in the bushes
around the library. I was locked out of my flat once.

Getting There

A penfriend living overseas wrote
me a letter telling me a bit about life there

how he too was a library assistant once
and that Mao Zedong was too. The City Librarian

told me that Philip Larkin was a librarian
and that I should think about getting

a library qualification. Work it out. I'm trying
to get my degree. Just nine papers after this year.

Witi Ihimaera wrote a short story about a young Maori
who took so many many years to get a degree

but in the end he got it and his whole whanau
were there to support him at graduation.

I've already planned mine. We'll take a photo
at the floral clock together, and smile a lot.

Sole Charge

Donald Kerr, the Rare Books Librarian,
went to North America for two months — which left

me alone with the collection. The first month
I spent doing more vacuuming and dusting, and

I finished a bibliography on the Kenderdine collection
of the *Rubaiyat of Omar Khayyam*. Then I started indexing

the photograph collection. One day I went up to morning
tea and while I was sipping coffee the fire alarm went off.

I dashed downstairs, and told everyone to clear the room.
This was okay. I checked everyone was out, locked

the doors, and assembled with the other staff outside.
The fire brigade gave the all clear to re-enter the building.

Just as I was about to unlock the doors and walk in,
a staff member noticed mist rolling out of the stack areas.

Blow me days. The CO_2 gas system had gone off without
warning. I would've opened the doors and been literally

extinguished, with some of the very best literature
in the land. What a tragic ending to the sequence eh!

Sir George

A bit of a character from all accounts. Loved
showing visitors his subtropical gardens at Kawau.

When we were putting the Autograph Letters display
together I read heaps of people speaking of Grey's

generosity, including Charles Darwin, and I think
he supported an expedition by Speke into the African

interior. In the Rossdhu Book of Hours there's
a miniature of St George slaying the dragon, which

we use on promotions and postcards, and I'm sure
Sir George derived pleasure from looking at it.

Whenever Grey visited London he'd always pop into
Bernard Quaritch and go on a spending splurge. The

great bulk of his collection went much earlier
to the South Africans in Cape Town, though we didn't

do too badly. I can understand the anger
that went into beheading his statue in Albert Park,

but the protestors could have focused their
worthy attention on the living. His name is in gold

above the honours board at Auckland Grammar School
which I attended for five years and remember mixedly.

The Onehunga Rare Books Assistant

Talking with a friend last night I had the idea
that I was really still, and that rooms, buildings,

people and objects would surround themselves
about me. I was in a world where everything

was visiting. I'm a bit egocentric. Born
and raised in Grafton until I was seven. Then

I moved to Onehunga, or vice versa. My home was
an old farmhouse transported to the suburb from Mangere,

made from a native timber, probably totara.
At home I ate a lot of scones, washed a lot of boots,

did a lot of homework. Read a lot of books.
As a kid I'd visit the Onehunga Public Library

to read about the Russian Revolution and the Roman Empire.
Sometimes at school I'd shelve books at lunchtime for fun.

Today, in my second week back on relief staff at Epsom,
I watched the documentary *The Mighty Civic*

and for some reason was reminded of a childhood full
of enchanted librarians combing shelves for me.